LOVE

GOD'S HEART

GRACE

WestBow
PRESS
A DIVISION OF THOMAS NELSON

WestBow Press books may be ordered through booksellers or by contacting:

WestBow Press
A Division of Thomas Nelson
1663 Liberty Drive
Bloomington, IN 47403
www.westbowpress.com
1-(866) 928-1240

Because of the dynamic nature of the Internet, any web addresses or links contained in this book may have changed since publication and may no longer be valid. The views expressed in this work are solely those of the author and do not necessarily reflect the views of the publisher, and the publisher hereby disclaims any responsibility for them.

Any people depicted in stock imagery provided by Thinkstock are models, and such images are being used for illustrative purposes only.

Certain stock imagery © Thinkstock.

Holy Bible, New Living Translation, copyright 1996, 2004 by Tyndale Charitable Trust.

The Merriam-Webster Dictionary, copyright 2004 by Merriam-Webster, Incorporated

ISBN: 978-1-4497-5211-8 (sc)
ISBN: 978-1-4497-5212-5 (e)

Library of Congress Control Number: 2012917793

Printed in the United States of America

WestBow Press rev. date: 11/07/2012

I would like to thank my Mother for showing me the Way, the Truth, and the Life …..The Lord Jesus.

GRACE

1ST <u>CORINTHIANS</u> 13

1. If I could speak in any language in heaven or on earth but didn't love others, I would only be making meaningless noise like a loud gong or a clanging cymbal. 2. If I had the gift of prophecy, and if I knew all the mysteries of the future and knew everything about everything, but didn't love others, what good would I be? And if I had the gift of faith so that I could speak to a mountain and make it move, without love I would be no good to anybody. 3. If I gave everything I have to the poor and even gave my body to be burned,* or sacrificed my body, I could boast about it; but if I didn't love others, I would be of no value whatsoever.

4. Love is patient and kind. Love is not jealous or boastful or proud 5. or rude. Love does not demand its own way. Love is not irritable, and it keeps no record of when it has been wronged. 6. It is never glad about injustice but rejoices whenever the truth wins out. 7. Love never gives up, never loses faith, is always hopeful, and endures through every circumstance.

8. Love will last forever, but prophecy and speaking in unknown languages,* or tongues, and special knowledge will all disappear. 9. Now we know only a little, and even the gift of prophecy reveals little! 10. But when the end comes, these special gifts will all disappear.

11. It's like this: When I was a child, I spoke and thought and reasoned as a child does. But when I grew up, I put away childish things. 12. Now we see things imperfectly as in a poor mirror, but then we will see face to face with perfect clarity. All that I know now is partial and incomplete, but then I will know everything completely, just as God knows me now.

13. There are three things that will endure--faith, hope, and love--and the greatest of these is love.

Table of Contents

Love Questions Everyone Asks

Can you touch love? Can you see love? Can you hear love? Can you smell or taste love?

Is love a feeling or emotion? Does love change? Is it unstable like everything else? Does love come and go?

Do you love some people more than others? Is love a "relationship?"

Is love something you do for someone else? Is it service to others?

Can you "love" yourself? What does that look like?

What does it look like when two people love each other? Between a man and woman? Between two friends?

Where does love come from?

Can you study "love?" Can you "learn" how to love others?

Is love a motivation? A power?

If I sacrificially lay down my life, care and serve others, is that love?

Is the greatest love and bond on earth between a mother and her child? A father and his child?

Does love die?

When someone I love hurts me, do I have to love them anymore? Does forgiveness have anything to do with love? Can two people who hate each other, learn to love each other?

Society says sex, relationships, and marriage are love—isn't that true love?

What about romance?

Are the songs, books, and television shows about true love?

Do all relationships end?

What about family, is that the greatest love on earth?

How can you tell if someone loves you?

Can two people 'fall in love?' Can two people 'fall out of love?'

Why does it hurt so much when love relationships die?

Why does it hurt so much when you say 'good-bye' to someone you love?

Does love come from the 'heart?' What is the 'heart?'

Is love just an emotion? Do we have spirits, souls, and bodies that need love?

What is the 'Spirit' of a person? Can that 'Spirit' bond with another 'Spirit?'

How important is love?

How can I show others that I love them?

Can you 'force' someone to love you?

Is it a 'choice' to love someone, or just an emotion that can't be controlled?

Is it just a matter of 'finding the right person?'

What does it 'feel' like when someone loves you?

When someone says, "I love you," how can I tell they are telling the truth?

Does love have, and what kind of, action?

What do I do if someone I love hates me?

Where do I turn, and what does it look like, to see true love?

Who is the greatest teacher of love the world has ever seen? Where do I find him or her?

How can I find a spouse that will love me forever?

Innocent children love and trust so much, when they are young. Why don't we trust and love like that when we are adults?

Does love need anything else to stay alive and be strong 'until death do us part?'

Is there any loyalty among people these days?

Where do I look for loyalty when I need someone to talk to?

Where can I find a loyal and faithful spouse?

How do I teach my children about love, loyalty, and faithfulness?

How do I teach my children to love, be faithful, loyal, and trustworthy to each other...to their spouses...and their children?

How do I teach my children about love, where to find it, and what it looks like?

What if my spouse/employer abuses me? What if I can't leave?

Am I supposed to 'love' my friends? And 'hate' my enemies?

Do I have the 'right to hate' someone who has hurt me?

What about strangers, the poor, the orphans, the fatherless, and the widow? Am I supposed to 'love' them? How do I 'love' those I do not know, or those I do not know well?

What about all the suffering in the world? Does one person make a difference? How do I get started?

What about the 'pan-handler' on the street? Is it wise to always give money?

I've heard a lot about fund raising for the poor and not one dime going to the poor. Who can I trust? What are some trustworthy options?

What about my x-spouse, do I have to 'love' him/her after all the damage and pain he/she caused me and my children?

Can love heal? Emotionally, mentally, physically, spiritually, and in relationships?

Divine Love

Is there 'Divine Love?'

Is there God's love on earth?

Is 'true love' alive on this mess of a planet, today? What is it and where do I find it?

How can I find this 'true love?'

I do not want to go to 'church' because of the hypocrisy and hurt. Does this mean God has rejected me and does not love me? Does this mean I can never find 'true love?'

Is there really a heaven and hell, and how can a loving God send people to hell?

Is it only in 'church' that I can find God's love?

The people in 'church' are just as sinful as those outside of 'church,' how can I ever find His 'Saints' and a way to heaven?

If God is like the people in 'church'—no thanks, I have enough hurt in my life. How can I ever be 'saved' and go to heaven?

Can God forgive everything I have done? Even the unpardonable sin? Does He even want to?

People in 'church' have the same problems everyone else on this messed up planet has. What can 'God and church' offer me?

Isn't God some kind of angry, punishing, never satisfied, unreliable, old judge? Isn't He waiting for me to die so He can judge and punish me? Isn't He counting up all my mistakes, ready to 'zap' me with some kind of punishment?

Or is God so weak that He allows people to hurt each other and not do anything about it?

What about all the innocent people starving and dying of disease and poverty? And most people do not even have clean water. What is a 'loving God' doing about that?

How can a 'loving God' allow my loved ones to suffer and die?

I thought God was more powerful than satan. I see more of satan's work than God's. I thought God was 'all powerful' and I see no justice at all. How can I believe He is a 'loving Father?'

How can I trust a God I do not understand, see, or feel?

Can I 'hear' this loving God, or do I need to rely on preachers, ministers, and priests?

How do I talk to this 'God of Love?' How and where do I find this 'God of Love?'

Will He make me poor and suffer if I trust Him?

Will He disown me and punish me if I make a mistake or sin before Him?

How can I touch, feel, see, hear, taste, and smell this God who is love?'

How do I know if some 'thing' or is some 'person' is from God?

How do I 'follow Christ?' Where do I begin? After following Christ for a while, how do I grow?

How do I know God is 'good' and how do I tell the difference between God's people and satan's people?

How do I know if something that happens to me, or my loved ones, is from God or satan?

Doesn't satan sometimes come as a 'Angel of Light?'

Does God ever lie? How do you know for sure that God never lies?

Does satan ever tell the truth?

How do I know that God loves me?

How do I know what His will is for me?

How do I know He wants to be the Father, Mother, husband, wife, or child I lost or never had?

What does God say about loneliness?

Should I be 'afraid' of God? What is the 'fear of the Lord?' Is that like 'fearing' a whipping from a parent?

What about war and starvation and poverty? Did God create that, too?

What is faith? What part of love does faith play? How do you get faith?

How much does God love me? Does He love everyone?

Will He ever abandon me for any reason like my spouse (mother, father, or child) did? How can I be sure?

What is prayer? How do you pray? What am I supposed to pray for? How often should I pray?

Does prayer work?

What if my prayers are unanswered? Does that mean God does not hear me? Does that mean God does not love me?

How do I pray for my needs? What if I am lost, hungry, thirsty, homeless, or lonely? Does God care about those things?

God is Love 1 John 4: 16

I will be answering these questions from a Biblical point of view. What does the Bible have to say about love? What did Jesus say? God is love and we need to look at Him to see what love is. His Word, the Bible, shows us clearly what love is. He is our Creator, and He created us to love and be loved.

Man's greatest need and desire is to love and be loved. It is the greatest motivator. This is the greatest truth in all of life, and God is the purest form of love. Our Creator designed us to love and be loved. And God is a Spirit so we, in this earthly form, cannot use our five senses to find love. We can read about love, touch others we love, see the service of love to others, and see the difference in life love can make, but love is a Spirit. God is a Spirit.

Let's take a closer look at 1st John 4: 16-5:5.

> _16. We know how much God loves us, and we have put our trust in His love. God is love, and all who live in love live in God, and God lives in them. 17. And as we live in God, our love grows more perfect. So we will not be afraid on the day of judgment, but we can face Him with confidence because we live like Jesus here in this world._

9

18. Such love has no fear, because perfect love expels all fear. If we are afraid, it is for fear of punishment, and this shows that we have not fully experienced His perfect love. 19. We love because He loved us first.

20. If someone says, "I love God," but hates a Christian brother or sister, that person is a liar; for if we don't love people we can see, how can we love God, whom we cannot see? 21. And He has given us this command: Those who love God must also love their Christian brothers and sisters.

5:1. Everyone who believes that Jesus is the Christ has become a child of God. And everyone who loves the Father loves His children, too. 2. We know we love God's children if we love God and obey His commandments. 3. Loving God means keeping His commandments, and His commandments are not burdensome. 4. For every child of God defeats this evil world, and we achieve this victory through our faith. 5. And who can win this battle against the world? Only those who believe that Jesus is the Son of God.

1st JOHN 4: 16-5: 5

That Scripture says a lot about love. John was called the 'Apostle of Love' because he wrote so much about love and the scriptures call him, John, "the Disciple Jesus loved."

Jesus loved everyone and He taught us not to love just our families and friends, but to love our enemies, too. And how do we love our fellow man? Jesus said to,

> *"Pray for those who persecute you! In that way, you will be acting as true children of your Father in heaven."*

MATTHEW 5: 43-45

"I know but, I just can't forgive that person because of the harm they did." We are commanded by the Lord Jesus to forgive. You cannot have love without forgiveness and you cannot have forgiveness without love. Forgiveness from the heart is crucial in loving others. When we forgive with our hearts fully, we will be able to have the hurt healed and we will forget.

"I thought sex and relationships were love. Isn't love what marriage is all about? And how do you know you love someone without living with them first?"

God made man and woman in His image. Adam and Eve were in a perfect garden, with no shame. But there was temptation, and they fell. Adam and Eve committed treason and bowed their knees to satan. They gave authority to satan and he became the 'god' of this earth and mankind now has to bow its knee to satan, until a person is born-again, into God's family. Once a person is born-again into God's family, then God can come into a person's spirit, soul, and body and begin the recovery of that person from a fallen state, blessed by God instead of cursed by satan. We are in the middle of a war between God and satan. Jesus won the victory and now it is a question of saving people from the god of this earth, satan.

When a man and woman marry it is for good. God did not make man and woman to be concerned about sex, marriage, and living together to 'try' each other out. God gave us marriage to be holy and sacred in His sight in spirit, soul, and body. All divorces are messy and out of the will of God. It hurts so much because your spirits, souls, and bodies are being torn apart. The intimacy of sex is for a married couple and not to be treated lightly. Children are not to be put in foster homes and forgotten. God loves and created the family. He even took great care to pass down the genealogies of many great Saints in His Word, the Bible. In the Bible many promises are given to us and 'our children.' God holds marriage and family dear to Him. It is a blessing that we must hold sacred, holy, and dear to us as God made man and woman for each other to enjoy a life-time together. From the Word of God we see the image of a loving God who wants to be our Father. If, because of divorce, you have no father or your father was abusive in your days of growing up, how will you know what 'a loving Father' is all about? Who protects you, makes sure you have the necessities of life, and teaches you about love from God's point of view? That's a Father's job on this earth. To teach us to respect, love, and admire our Heavenly Father. The bible, God's Word to us, says we are to keep our bodies as a sacrifice, holy, and acceptable to Him in Roman's 12:1, 2. Let's take a look at those two verses in Romans.

> 1.And so, dear Christian friends, I plead with you to give your bodies to God. Let them be a living and holy sacrifice—the kind he will accept. When you think of what he has done for you, is this too much to ask? 2. Don't copy the behavior and customs of this world, <u>but let God transform you into a new person by changing the way you think. Then you will know what God wants you to do, and you will know how good and pleasing and perfect His will really is.</u>

ROMANS 12:1, 2

Our bodies are meant to be the Temple of God, a home for the Father, Son, and the Holy Spirit. That's why pornography and all sexual sins are so devastating. Not only does it destroy the beholder, but if you follow the lives of those who indulge, it destroys everyone concerned. I have seen the end of lives of those who did not repent from sexual sin and what that does. It is devastating, like alcoholism and drug addiction, except worse. It leads to homelessness, divorce, perversions, loss of family and friends, and all kinds of other problems. Our bodies were meant to house the Spirit of the Lord and be useful for worship, work, fellowship, and having children. Intimacy and sex is for the married couple. And marriage was created for one man and one woman, like Adam and Eve in the garden. This is one reason our culture is so immoral, because we have not been responsible with our bodies. We have not held dear our sexual 'powers' over each other and we have almost destroyed our society. That is one big reason 'love' in our society is so hard to define. We have no idea what 'true love' is! Now, our society is so perverted, that we have to have 'love' defined. We believe that marriage is true love and divorce is 'no fault', we had nothing to do with it, it 'just happened.' And is so common! The ripping and tearing of our spirits, souls, and bodies in divorce is now common and we do not even shed a tear. And, the death of an unborn child, is now common. Abortion is now as common as pulling a tooth at the dentist's office. We, as a society, have made sex between the unmarried so common that if there is an unplanned pregnancy, we just go and kill the child. <u>ABORTION IS NOT LOVE!!! SEX OUTSIDE OF MARRIAGE AND LIVING TOGETHER WITHOUT COMMITMENT IS NOT LOVE!!!!</u> And now we are facing human trafficking. Most human traffickers take innocent children and make them have sex with strangers, 20-30 times a day, and they take little girls and little boys. Slavery is now more common than ever before! There are literally millions of people in slavery today. This is all born out of the sexual sin that we ignore in our society today. What can I do? I am only one.

It only takes one to reverse the tide for millions. Think of how many children in extreme poverty are being fed by James and Betty Robison. They gave their lives to God and listened to Him. Now, they are making a difference in millions of people's lives. But, they started out with a Bible, and a determination to serve Him, no matter the cost. And there are others who have sacrificed themselves to serve God. What about Mother Theresa, and the Salvation Army? They all started with only their Bible and a determination to serve God, wherever He led. Another famous person is Billy Graham. One person can make a difference. In the Bible there are countless people who kept their bodies holy and did wonderful things for others, especially our great example, Christ Himself. He showed us what a life sacrificed to God could do and what God's will is, today, in this life. This is how love is seen and felt. What does it mean when someone brings you food when there is nothing growing in your country? What does it mean when someone rescues you from a life of slavery, gives you protection, teaches you a skill, and introduces you to Jesus, who is 'Love?'

What about the person who was 'different' and 'peculiar,' because they said "No," to your advances, drugs, alcohol, and other things that were 'normal' for you and your friends? Didn't you wonder what was so 'different' about them? True Christians are 'different' and 'peculiar' people. They are loved by God and have a reason to live and say "no" to the things of this world that are 'normal' for most people. The true Christian does not 'bow their knee' to the 'god' of this world, satan. Because they have 'tasted' true love and want nothing else. I am NOT saying the true Christian is perfect. We are a 'work in progress,' but the mature Christian has outgrown and turned his back on the things of this world. And God forgives his children when they ask and repent. God can and will forgive and save you if you repent and ask Him to be your Lord and Master. He always has an outstretched hand toward the poor, the needy, the hurting, the confused, and the seeking. He will hear your prayer and change you if you ask. I promise. Just say a prayer, bow your head and from your heart, ask Him to forgive you and change your life. He will. He is waiting.

God is not just trustworthy and reliable, but also: tenderhearted, slow to anger and full of mercy, kind, humble, honest, faithful, kindhearted, meek, tender, forgiving, merciful, loving, imaginative, all-knowing, and all-powerful. All this is shown in His Word, the Bible. In His Word, He is also seen as self-sacrificing, and madly in love with us.

> *16.For God so loved the world that he gave his only Son, so that everyone who believes in Him will not perish but have eternal life. 17. God did not send his Son into the world to condemn it, but to save it.*

> JOHN 3: 16, 17

The Character of God

It is not just enough to know that "God is love." Let's take a closer look at God to see what His love looks like. Many places in the New Testament Jesus said, "Fear not." God does not want to harm us. God is good. To see this, let's look at the 112th and 113th Psalms.

> *Praise the Lord! Happy are those who fear the Lord. Yes, happy are those who delight in doing what He commands. 2. Their children will be successful everywhere; an entire generation of godly people will be blessed. 3. They themselves will be wealthy, and their good deeds will never be forgotten. 4. When darkness overtakes the godly, light will come bursting in. They are generous, compassionate, and righteous. 5. All goes well for those who are generous, who lend freely and conduct their business fairly. 6. Such people will not be overcome by evil circumstances. Those who are righteous will be long remembered. 7. They do not fear bad news, they confidently trust the Lord to care for them. 8. They are confident and fearless and can face their foes triumphantly. 9. They give generously to those in need. Their good deeds will never be forgotten. They will have influence and honor. 10. The wicked will be infuriated when they see this. They will grind their teeth in anger; they will slink away, their hopes thwarted.*

> *PSALM 112*

Praise the Lord! Yes, give praise, O servants of the Lord. Praise the name of the Lord! 2. Blessed be the name of the Lord forever and ever. 3. Everywhere-from east to west- praise the name of the Lord. 4. For the Lord is high above the nations; His glory is far greater than the heavens. 5. Who can be compared with the Lord our God, who is enthroned on high? 6. Far below Him are the heavens and the earth. He stoops to look, 7. and He lifts the poor from the dirt and the needy from the garbage dump. 8. He sets them among princes, even the princes of His own people! 9. He gives the barren woman a home, so that she becomes a happy mother. Praise the Lord!

PSALM 113

These scriptures show God's Will and Promised Blessings. From the two Psalms above we see things that give us a clue to what God is like. He is good. *His will and promises are for our own benefit. You can see wealth, righteousness, generosity, fame, a home and family. These are things that everyone wants and spends their whole life trying to have, but the Bible says that God gives us these things freely.* As we trust and get to know God better and better, He gives us the blessings of life. Even protection and revenge are promised by God in Psalm 91. God is good. And He gives these blessings to those that follow and serve Him. But doesn't God ask us to suffer? NO! We suffer because we are not wise and make our own mistakes. Sometimes God will ask us to give up some things, but He promises to give them back and more, if we trust and follow Him.

29. "And everyone who has given up houses or brothers or sisters or father or mother or children or property, for my sake, will receive a hundred times as much in return and will have eternal life." Jesus

MATTHEW 19: 20

God is faithful, He keeps His promises. He cannot lie. If God were to say, "Today is Thursday." Then today would be Thursday. If God were to say, "You now have 7 fingers on your right hand." Look down, because you now have 7 fingers on your right hand. He is God and what He says is done. You can count on His every word being true. And the bible, is His Word and promises. It is the only thing in life you can count on. No man or woman, no institution, no country or its leaders can be counted on. We all break our promises. God does not. He is not a liar. Satan is the liar and he is the father of all lies. God is truth. The Bible spans over 6,000 years and what He has said has come true. All His promises are either fulfilled, are being fulfilled, or will be. You can count on what God says in His Word. He is trustworthy. He is the only one that can be counted on from now until eternity. If God is love, then why are some suffering and most will be going to eternal suffering and torment in hell?

The War: God and satan

First there was God. He has always been and will always be. He is eternal. He made the Angels and all physical existence. One day, one of the leading, most beautiful and musical angel, decided to exalt himself above God. His name was Lucifer, he led a rebellion and one-third of the angels were cast out of heaven. Lucifer became satan and became the exact opposite of God. Where God is love, satan is fear and hatred. Where God blesses people, satan curses them.

Later, God decided to have a family. He made Adam and Eve. They were Spirits, had souls, and lived in bodies as all mankind, their descendants. He made us in His image or likeness. God placed Adam and Eve in a perfect garden with all manner of plants and animals for blessings. All God asked was that they not eat from one tree, the tree of knowledge of good and evil. That was the only command God wanted honored.

Satan came to Eve and tempted her to eat of the forbidden fruit, she ate and gave some to Adam. They sinned. They bowed their knee and obeyed satan instead of God. Therefore, being the Mother and Father of all mankind, they brought a curse on all people and all creation. Mankind, the earth, the plants, the animals, and all creation suffers from that one disobedient act. From the time of the Garden of Eden, until Jesus died, we had no hope of deliverance from wicked satan and the curse.

Jesus came and lived a perfect sinless life. He was then sacrificed on the Cross to destroy the curse. Jesus went into hell and suffered so that we would not have to. At the end of three days, God raised Jesus from the dead and Jesus defeated satan and all of hell. Jesus defeated death and the grave.

So, from one man's sin, Adam, came all evil. And from one man's perfect obedience, Jesus, came forgiveness, restoration, and all blessings. God is a faith being. It takes faith to please Him. Praying and accepting Jesus, His work on the cross, into your heart moves you from the kingdom of satan to the Kingdom of God.

Jesus coming to earth and suffering to save us from satan, death, the grave, hell, and all curses is the greatest act of love ever displayed. His life and sacrifice to save us is the most powerful form of love in existence. And the war has been won by Jesus. Satan is a defeated enemy. Now the Commission is to save as many as possible while there is still time. And equip those disciples to rescue as many as possible with the good news of Jesus. It is God's will all be saved.

Faith

Love is the commitment to be faithful and honor your spouse throughout life. Love is caring for the widow, the fatherless, the poor, and the stranger. Love is healing the broken heart and broken body. Love is giving clean water and food to those who have none. Love is bringing harmony in a home. Love is teaching right from wrong. Love is thinking pure, lovely, honorable thoughts and encouraging others with faith-filled words.

Our words decide our destinies. We are: either speaking love and blessings, or we are speaking curses on ourselves and others. Listen to your words, this is faith. Do you have faith in God and His love? Or are you speaking fear and curses on yourself and those around you? Your words are coming from your heart. What you think about gets down into your heart. If you meditate on God's Word and God Himself, your heart and thoughts will be pure and your mouth will speak blessings. Do you have forgiveness in your heart? Or are you hanging on to bitterness, anger, hurt, hate, fear, death, and doubt? Listen to your own words and what the people around you are saying. Our thoughts and what we meditate on decide our destinies. This is faith. We either believe the best or expect the worst.

33. "A tree is identified by its fruit. Make a tree good, and its fruit will be good. Make a tree bad, and its fruit will be bad. 34.

> *You brood of snakes! How could evil men like you speak what is good and right? For whatever is in your heart determines what you say. 35. A good person produces good words from a good heart, and an evil person produces evil words from an evil heart. 36. And I tell you this that you must give an account on judgment day of every idle word you speak. 37. The words you say now reflect your fate then, either you will be justified by them or you will be condemned." Jesus*

MATTHEW 12: 33-37

God is Spirit and He creates and rules by faith. He is a faith being. That is why He created speech for us and gave us the promises through His Word, the Bible. *All answers for life, goodness, righteousness, love, humility, marriage, raising children, finances, relationships, service, heaven, and hell He gave us through His Word. All His promises and character, HIS HEART, is found in His Word and God is love.We are made in His image and likeness so we are to speak faith words from our heart, too. The Spirit realm, which rules over the physical, is operated by faith. The words that come from our heart, gives power to the spirit world to change the physical. That is faith.* And what we think and meditate on gets down into our heart and it comes out of our mouth. The words coming out of our mouth moves the spirit world to decide our destiny. It affects everyone and everything around us. This is true for us in this life on earth and judgment after death. All eternity is based on our words today.

Listen to your own thoughts and words. Listen to those around you. Do you hear sickness? Do you hear "damnation?" Do you hear words of death or "hell?" Do you hear the Lord's name taken in vain or as a curse word? Do you swear? Do the people around you swear? Do you curse God with "damnation?" Or maybe you do not swear, but talk sickness and disease? Do you talk to people about how "poor you are?" How you "hurt all over?" Do you vote? Or talk about how dishonest our leaders are? Do you pray for our leaders?

About 2,000 years ago James, the half-brother of Jesus, wrote and spoke much about the tongue.

> *2. We all make many mistakes, but those who control their tongues can also control themselves in every other way. 3. We can make a large horse turn around and go wherever we want by means of a small bit in its mouth. 4. And a tiny rudder makes a huge ship turn wherever the pilot wants it to go, even though the winds are strong. 5. So also, the tongue is a small thing, but what enormous damage it can do. A tiny tongue is a flame of fire. It is full of wickedness that can ruin your whole life. It can turn the entire course of your life into a blazing flame of destruction, for it is set on fire by hell itself.*

> *7. People can tame all kinds of animals and birds and reptiles and fish, 8. But no one can tame the tongue. It is an uncontrollable evil, full of deadly poison. 9. Sometimes it praises our Lord and Father, and sometimes it breaks out into curses against those who have been made in the image of God. 10. And so blessing and cursing come pouring out of the same mouth. Surely, my brothers and sisters, this is not right! 11. Does a spring of water bubble out with both fresh water and bitter water? 12. Can you pick olives from a fig tree or figs from a grapevine? No, and you can't draw fresh water from a salty pool.*

> *JAMES 3: 2-12*

God wants us to love Him and each other so He gave us His Word. We have gone from the kingdom of darkness and have been translated into the Kingdom of light, if we have been born-again. Therefore, let's practice loving, faith-filled words that encourage ourselves and others around us. In prayer, ask the Holy Spirit to tame your tongue and fill your heart with love for God and His children. Meditate on the Word to renew your mind. Your heart will become pure and your words will bless everyone and everything around you.

There is <u>power</u> in the words you speak. Jesus talked about this.

> *22 .Then Jesus said to the disciples, "Have faith in God. 23. I assure you that you can say to this mountain, 'May God lift you up and throw you into the sea,' and your command will be obeyed. All that's required is that you really believe and do not doubt in your heart. 24. Listen to me! You can pray for anything, and if you believe, you will have it. 25. But when you are praying, first forgive anyone you are holding a grudge against, so that your Father in heaven will forgive your sins, too. 26. But if you do not forgive, neither will your Father who is in heaven forgive your sins.*

> MARK 11: 22-26

A lot of Christians try to change things by speaking words. That is not faith. Words alone cannot change things. It is faith in our heart, planted by God's Word and fellowship with Him, that produces faith.

"Faith comes by hearing and hearing by the Word of God."

> ROMANS 10: 17

It is in hearing and studying and meditating on the Word that makes faith grow. Then the words of faith that changes things, comes naturally.

God's Will-Blessings

'Bless' is defined in the Merriam-Webster Dictionary as "to invoke divine care for," or, "to confer happiness upon." 'Blessed,' is defined as 'Delightful.' And 'Blessing' is defined as "APPROVAL," or "a thing conductive to happiness." It is God's will we be cared for by Him and to have his approval, which gives us happiness.

God's promises throughout His Word shows He wants to bless us in every area of life. Deuteronomy 28: 1-14 shows us an example of this. God began giving all mankind a choice of Blessing or cursing when He brought His people out of slavery in Egypt and led them to the land He had promised Abraham. We have the choice of fulfilling the command of love and being blessed or living selfishly and receiving curses. Let's take a look at some of the Blessings God promised when we fulfill the commandments of love stated in both the Old and New Testaments.

> "If you fully obey the Lord your God by keeping all the commands I am giving you today, the Lord your God will exalt you above all the nations of the world. 2. You will experience all these Blessings if you obey the Lord your God:
>
> 3. You will be blessed in your towns and in the country.

4. You will be blessed with many children and productive fields.

You will be blessed with fertile herds and flocks.

5. You will be blessed with baskets overflowing with fruit, and with kneading bowls filled with bread.

6. You will be blessed wherever you go, both in coming and in going.

7. "The Lord will conquer your enemies when they attack you. They will attack you from one direction, but they will scatter from you in seven!

8. "The Lord will bless everything you do and will fill your storehouses with grain. The Lord your God will bless you in the land he is giving you.

9. If you obey the commands of the Lord your God and walk in his ways, the Lord will establish you as his holy people as he solemnly promised to do. 10. Then all the nations of the world will see that you are a people claimed by the Lord, and they will stand in awe of you.

11. "The Lord will give you an abundance of good things in the land he swore to give your ancestors—many children, numerous livestock, and abundant crops. 12. The Lord will send rain at the proper time from his rich treasury in the heavens to bless all the work you do. You will lend to many nations, but you will never need to borrow from them. 13. If you listen to these commands of the Lord your God and carefully obey them, the Lord will make you the head and not the tail, and you will always have the upper hand. 14. You must not turn away from any of the commands I am giving you today to follow after other gods and worship them.

Deuteronomy 28: 1- 14

We have already seen the promises in Psalms 112 and 113, and there are more promises in Isaiah 54. All through God's Word; He promises to love and care for us. Are there any 'strings attached?' Yes! Jesus made all the commandments of God simple for us.

> *37. Jesus replied, "'You must love the Lord your God with all your heart, all your soul, and all your mind.' 38. This is the first and greatest commandment. 39. A second is equally important: 'Love your neighbor as yourself.' 40. All the other commandments and all the demands of the prophets are based on these two commandments."*

> MATTHEW 22: 37- 40

God is love and all He asks us to do is love Him, our fellow man, and ourselves. It is that simple. And how do we know if we are fulfilling that command? A 'guide' is the Ten Commandments, Deuteronomy 5: 7-21. We are to love God enough not to worship any other idols or make idols. We will not take His name in vain. We will love Sundays and want to worship Him with other Christians. We will want to honor our parents and respect them. We will not commit murder, nor commit adultery, but be faithful to our spouse. If we are loving God, and our fellow man, we will not steal or lie. If we are being taken care of by the Blessing of the Lord, there will be no need for covetousness.If we are fulfilling the law of love the Ten Commandments will automatically be fulfilled. And after the Ten Commandments, we have the Sermon on the Mount by Jesus to guide us in love, Matthew Chapters 5-7.

Jesus came to remove the curse and so we would not only be born-again and spend eternity in heaven, but He also suffered so we would not have to in this life-time on earth.

> *10. "The thief's purpose is to steal, and kill, and destroy. My purpose is to give life in all its fullness. I am the good shepherd. The good shepherd lays down His life for the sheep." Jesus.*

> JOHN 10: 10-11

This is love. This is how we know the difference between faith and fear. We can know the difference between good and evil, right and wrong, love and hate by God's Word. We can ask in each and every situation, "What does God's Word say?" "What did Jesus say?" "What did God do?" What did Jesus do?" By God's Word we can always know the difference between God's love and blessings and the enemies' destruction. Now, let's take a look at a few of God's Blessings, His will for us.

God's Will—Healing

One of the blessings is healing. It is for us physically, as well as our soul, heart, and mind. This healing goes from the top of our head through the soles of our feet, through our soul (which is our mind and emotions), from our Spirit. God wants us healthy, strong, youthful, and whole: spirit, soul, and body. We see these promises in three major scriptures.

> *27. O Israel, how can you say the Lord does not see your troubles? How can you say God refuses to hear your case? 28. Have you never heard or understood? Don't you know that the Lord is the everlasting God, the Creator of all the earth? He never grows faint or weary. No one can measure the depths of his understanding. 29. He gives power to those who are tired and worn out; he offers strength to the weak. 30. Even youths will become exhausted, and young men will give up. 31. But those who wait on the Lord will find new strength. They will fly high on wings like eagles. They will run and not grow weary. They will walk and not faint.*
>
> Isaiah 40: 27- 31

4. Yet it was our weaknesses he carried; it was our sorrows,*sicknesses he carried, it was our diseases that weighed him down. And we thought his troubles were a punishment from God for his own sins! 5. But he was wounded and crushed for our sins. He was beaten that we might have peace. He was whipped, and we were healed! 6. All of us have strayed away like sheep. We have left God's paths to follow or own. Yet the Lord laid on him the guilt and sins of us all.

ISAIAH 53: 4- 6

24. He personally carried away our sins in his own body on the cross so we can be dead to sin and live for what is right. You have been healed by his wounds! 25. Once you were wandering like lost sheep. But now you have turned to your Shepherd, the Guardian of your souls.

1ˢᵗ PETER 2: 24, 25

What if I am not healed?

We have to accept our healing the same way we accepted Jesus into our heart when we were born—again. It is by faith. We need to listen to the Word preached about healing, spend time in His Word, prayer, and fellowship with God. As the Word and presence of God grows stronger we can exercise our faith by asking God for healing and by speaking healing from our heart. Our faith in His Word and promises brings about the healing we need. BUT, WE MUST WATCH OUR WORDS! Our victory or defeat comes from our words. Are we convinced of our healing enough to fight off and resist the enemy? Or do we given in and say what we 'feel,' or what the 'doctor said?'

Miracles happen today just as they did when Jesus walked the earth.

5b. "I will never fail you. I will never forsake you."

6. That is why we can say with confidence, "The Lord is my helper, so I will not be afraid. What can mere mortals do to me?"

8. Jesus Christ is the same yesterday, today, and forever.

HEBREWS 12: 5b, 6, 8

Jesus has always healed anyone who came to Him in faith. Not one time, did Jesus ever say, "No." And Jesus healed thousands of people— no matter what the illness was.

17. When they came down the slopes of the mountain, the disciples stood with Jesus on a large, level area, surrounded by many of his followers and by the crowds. There were people from all over Judea and from Jerusalem and from as far north as the seacoasts of Tyre and Sidon. 18. They had come to hear him and to be healed, and Jesus cast out many evil spirits. <u>19. Everyone was trying to touch him, because healing power went out from him, and they were all cured</u>.

LUKE 6: 17- 19

There were thousands of people Jesus healed with all kinds of diseases and illnesses. Handicapped, lame, crippled, blind, deaf, paralyzed, and even missing limbs grew back just by touching Him. ANY AND EVERY ONE WAS MADE PHYSICALLY WHOLE!! Remember, Jesus is the same yesterday, today, and forever, and it was by His wounds we were healed!

Meditate on the Word beginning with Isaiah 53, 1 Peter 2: 24, and wherever Jesus healed people. The faith to be healed <u>will </u>come. Find teaching tapes on healing. Kenneth and Gloria Copeland out of Ft. Worth, Texas, and Rheama from Tulsa, Oklahoma have good strong healing materials. DO NOT LISTEN TO ANY ONE WHO SAYS THAT HEALING PASSED AWAY, BECAUSE IT HAS NOT!!!

I have been healed many times. I have been healed of torn ligaments, torn tendons, stomach trouble, typhoid fever, mental illness, a sprained back, alcoholism, drug addiction, I have lost 102 lbs., pinched nerve, muscle spasms, charley horses, and even a broken foot. These are just a few of the things God has healed me of. I cannot remember all the things I have been healed of. Jesus is still the same.

Do not allow the enemy to steal your miracle of healing. After you have a witness of the Holy Spirit in your heart and a scripture to stand on, claim your healing miracle verbally, out loud, <u>and do not turn loose with your words!!</u> Keep feeding your Spirit, soul, and body the Word of God, resisting the devil, and never give up. The Lord always heals when we ask and stand in faith!

> *7. So humble yourselves before God. Resist the Devil, and he will flee from you. 8. Draw close to God, and God will draw close to you.*

> JAMES 4: 7, 8

Ask God to heal you and then, tell the devil, <u>out loud</u>, "According to James 4:7 I am resisting you satan, so take your filthy hands off my body, mind, and emotions! In Jesus' precious name and blood!" And then begin<u>, out loud</u>, to thank God for healing you. Give Him thanks and glory for your healing. And do not stop until your healing is manifested in the physical. This is called, faith.

This is also the way you pray for your beloved. First, get your thoughts and heart on God and His Word. Pick out a scripture of healing God seems to be speaking to you through. Ask God to heal your loved one, or yourself, and resist the devil. After you have rebuked satan with the Word, begin thanking and praising God for your loved one's healing. And DO NOT STOP THANKING AND PRAISING HIM!!!

God's Will—Prosperity

22. *"The blessing of the Lord makes a person rich, and he adds no sorrow with it."*

PROVERBS 10: 22

22. *"A greedy person tries to get rich quick, but it only leads to poverty."*

PROVERBS 28: 22

25. *"Greed causes fighting; trusting the Lord leads to prosperity."*

PROVERBS 28: 25

27. *"Whoever gives to the poor will lack nothing. But a curse will come upon those who close their eyes to poverty."*

PROVERBS 28: 27

Almost all of us, when we hear the word "prosperity", we think of money. Money is just a part of that blessing but not all of it. Prosperity is also having a large, healthy, born—again family, houses, good crops and food to eat, peace, rain, and everything you need to get the Good News of Jesus to every creature on earth. *Is it God's will we be blessed financially? Yes! But not for our own selfish desires! We are blessed financially to do God's will on earth.*

> 27. *"Pure and lasting religion in the sight of God our Father means that we must care for orphans and widows in their troubles, and refuse to let the world corrupt us."*

> JAMES 1: 27

God will <u>not</u> grant us a lot of money just because we ask, especially if we are baby Christians and foolish with what we have. God trains His 'cheerful givers' for more blessing of finances. As we grow in the Lord and wisdom and faithfulness, God will trust us with more. As we show ourselves as trustworthy with what God has given us in His Word, faith, and in giving, He then grants us more. *Giving wisely and praying for others prosperity are two of the keys.* Keeping it for our own selfish gain will bring poverty.

> 6. *Remember this—a farmer who plants only a few seeds will get a small crop. But the one who plant generously will get a generous crop. 7. You must each make up your own mind as to how much you should give. Don't give reluctantly or in response to pressure. For God loves the person who gives cheerfully. 8. And God will generously provide all you need. Then you will always have everything you need and plenty left over to share with others. 9. As the Scriptures say,*

> *"Godly people give generously to the poor.*

> *Their good deeds will never be forgotten."*

10. for God is the one who gives seed to the farmer and then bread to eat. In the same way, he will give you many opportunities to do good, and he will produce a great harvest of generosity in you.

2 CORINTHIANS 9: 6—10

It also takes wisdom to prosper. In all areas of life, from raising children to knowing a skill for work, it takes wisdom to prosper. <u>And wisdom comes from meditating in the Word and doing what it says.</u>

10. "Bring all the tithes into the storehouse so there will be enough food in my Temple. If you do," says the Lord Almighty, "I will open the windows of heaven for you. I will pour out a blessing so great you won't have enough room to take it in! Try it! Let me prove it to you! 11. Your crops will be abundant, for I will guard them from insects, and disease. Your grapes will not shrivel before they are ripe," says the Lord Almighty. 12. "Then all nations will call you blessed, for your land will be such a delight," says the Lord Almighty.

MALACHI 3: 10—12

We can start by tithing. The tithe is holy and decides if you are blessed or cursed. And if you will meditate on the book of Malachi, you will find your words are important here, too!

Deuteronomy 26 gives us examples of faith-filled love words we are to honor God with over our tithes and offerings. There is more to the tithe than just quickly writing a check or giving some cash in the Sunday service. God wants our hearts and souls. He has plenty of cash already. He created it. He wants us. He wants our devotion, worship, gratitude, and service in every area of life. He wants to be Lord over our hearts as well as our finances. <u>If you want to see where your heart is, look to see where your money is.</u>

When we worship money we are living like the world. Do you think of money constantly?

Are you worried about your finances? Are you greedy or horde money and material things? Do you ever give to the poor above your tithes to your church? It does not matter if you are rich or poor every one of us is tested in the area of finances. Do you worry, or do you search God's Word for direction? Do you pray for others to be blessed financially? Do you pray for others' needs to be met?

Once we find in God's Word how to be blessed and we are living up to what we know, we can fellowship with our Heavenly Father and He can teach us more. More light equals more blessing. And whether it is money or healing or our children's salvation, we must stand in faith and watch our words! It takes faith, our words and attitude agreeing with God's Word and will, to bring about any and all miracles! God is a faith being. He moves, creates, judges, and works by faith.

> 20. *"You didn't have enough faith," Jesus told them. "I assure you, even if you had faith as small as a mustard seed you could say to this mountain, 'Move from here to there,' and it would move. Nothing would be impossible."*

> MATTHEW 17: 20

Humility and honesty is weighed greatly when we talk of prosperity. Yes, we must have faith for finances as well as any other need or promise, but also God wants us to be rich in character and in living good, honest lives. Even Proverbs says that if you do not work, you do not eat. The Apostle Paul was a tent-maker and never was dependent on the churches for his support. They gave to him from grateful hearts.

> 3. *As God's messenger, I give each of you this warning: Be honest in your estimate of yourselves, measuring your value by how much faith God has given you. 4. Just as our bodies have many parts and each part has a special function, 5. so it is with Christ's body. We are all parts of his one body, and*

each of us has different work to do. And since we are all one body in Christ, we belong to each other, and each of us needs all the others.

ROMANS 12: 3—5

It is not what we see, hear, feel, taste, or smell that counts for us to claim God's Blessings, it is our faith. And this works in the area of prosperity, too! Watch what you meditate on and say with your mouth.

Are you talking about inflation, taxes, and how hard it is to make a living? Are you talking about how, "you just do not know what you are going to do?" Are you talking about, "how high the unemployment rate is?" And, "how many are out of a job?" Are you saying, "It could happen to any one of us!" Do you have a paralyzing fear of losing your job and the economy? Are you afraid of homelessness and poverty? Fear was Job's secret sin.

Or, are you talking about, "How good God is?" Are you talking about, "His promises of care and provision?" Are you saying things about, "His faithfulness and your gratitude for how much He has given you and your family?" Are you searching God's Word daily for His protection and provision? *Are you carefully obeying His requirements of Love and giving? Are you meditating on His Word night and day?* Or watching T.V.?

> *8. Study this Book of the Law continually. Meditate on it day and night so you may be sure to obey all that is written in it. Only then will you succeed. 9. I command you—be strong and courageous! Do not be afraid or discouraged. For the Lord your God is with you wherever you go."*

JOSHUA 1: 8, 9

God's Will—Protection

Protection is guaranteed in God's Blessings, just as much as healing or prosperity. But, like all other promises, it takes faith to receive it. Are you talking about, "How dangerous your neighborhood is?" Are you talking about, "How dangerous the roads are?" Do you have insurance policies for every disaster you can imagine? Let's take a look at God's promises of protection. Psalm 91 is also known as the 'soldier's prayer,' and Isaiah 54 has something to say, too.

1. *Those who live in the shelter of the Most High will find rest in the shadow of the Almighty.*

2. *This I declare of the Lord: He alone is my refuge, my place of safety; he is my God, and I am trusting him.*

3. *For he will rescue you from every trap and protect you from the fatal plague.*

4. *He will shield you with his wings. He will shelter you with his feathers. His faithful promises are your armor and protection.*

5. *Do not be afraid of the terrors of the night, nor fear the dangers of the day,*

6.   Nor dread the plague that stalks in darkness, nor the disaster that strikes at midday.

7.   Though a thousand fall at your side, though ten thousand are dying around you, these evils will not touch you.

8.   But you will see it with your eyes; you will see how the wicked are punished.

9.   If you make the Lord your refuge, if you make the Most High your shelter,

10. no evil will conquer you; no plague will come near your dwelling.

11. For he orders his angels to protect you wherever you go.

12. They will hold you with their hands to keep you from striking your foot on a stone.

13. You will trample down lions and poisonous snakes; you will crush fierce lions and serpents under your feet! (demons)

14. The Lord says, "I will rescue those who love me. I will protect those who trust in my name.

15. When they call on me, I will answer; I will be with them in trouble. I will rescue them and honor them.

16. I will satisfy them with a long life and give them my salvation."

PSALM 91

You will live under a government that is just and fair. Your enemies will stay far away; you will live in peace. Terror will not come near. 15. If any nation comes to fight you, it will not be because I sent them to punish you. Your enemies will always be defeated because I am on your side. 16. I have created the blacksmith who fans the coals beneath the forge and makes the weapons of destruction. And I have created the armies that destroy. 17. But in that coming day (now), no weapon turned against you will succeed. And everyone who tells lies in court will be brought to justice. These benefits are enjoyed by the servants of the Lord; their vindication will come from me. I, the Lord, have spoken!

ISAIAH 54: 14-17

Any soldier on a field of battle has to have God's protection and we are Christ's body on earth. Even the Apostle Paul wrote about our prayer armor in Ephesians 6. Our battles are not with flesh and blood, but with the power of prayer, courage, and God's Word.

God's Will—Family

God wanted a family. That is why He created us in the first place. He wanted to *lavishly* pour out His love on sons and daughters. He has no grandchildren. We are Princes and Princesses in the Father God's Kingdom. We are heirs to His throne. We have thrones waiting for us in His sanctuary. We can *boldly* go into the Throne Room of the Most High, and make our requests and heart's desires known, to the One who rules and reigns over all! *What an honor*!! We are not just servants but *royalty!!*

The way I claim God's promises is to say the scriptures with my name and my beloved's names inserted. For example:

> 5. *Who can be compared with the Lord our God, who is enthroned on high? 6. Far below him are the heavens and the earth. He stoops to look, 7. and he lifts <u>me</u> from the dirt and the garbage dump. 8. He has set <u>me</u> among princes, even the princes of his own people! 9. He gave <u>me</u> a home, so that I became a happy mother. I praise the Lord!*
>
> PSALM 113: 5—9

This next scripture, in Isaiah, promises me that my children will be saved!

"But now, listen to me, <u>Grace</u> my servant, <u>Grace</u> my chosen one. 2. The Lord who made you and helps you says, O <u>Grace</u>, my servant, do not be afraid. O <u>Beloved Grace</u>, my chosen one, do not fear. 3. For I will give you abundant water to quench your thirst and to moisten your parched fields. And I will pour out my Spirit and my blessings on your children. 4. They will thrive like watered grass, like willows on a riverbank. 5. Some will proudly claim, 'I belong to the Lord.' Others will say, 'I am a descendant of Jacob.' Some will write the Lord's name on their hands and will take the honored name of Israel as their own."

ISAIAH 44: 1—5

And God gave me this promise ten years before my son was born.

"Sing, O childless woman! Break forth into loud and joyful song, O <u>Grace</u>, even though you never gave birth to a child. For you, the woman who could bear no children now has more than all the other women," says the Lord. (I now have ten 'Compassion Children' through Compassion International and my son, who is grown. That is eleven children I love.) 2. "Enlarge your house; build an addition; spread out your home! 3. For you, <u>Grace</u>, will soon be bursting at the seams. Your descendants will take over other nations and live in their cities. (My son is a soldier in the army.)

4. Fear not; <u>Grace</u>, you will no longer live in shame. The shame of your youth and the sorrows of widowhood (or divorce) will be remembered no more, 5. For your Creator will be your husband. The Lord Almighty is his name! He is your Redeemer, the Holy One of Israel, the God of all the earth. 6. For the Lord has called <u>me back from my grief</u>—as though I was a young wife abandoned by her husband," says your God. 7. "For a brief moment I abandoned you, but with great compassion I will take you back. 8. In a moment of anger I *turned my face away for a little while. But with everlasting love I will have compassion on you, <u>Grace</u>, says the Lord, your Redeemer.*

9. "Just as I swore in the time of Noah that I would never again let a flood cover the earth and destroy its life, so now I swear that I will never again pour out my anger on you, <u>Grace</u>. 10. For the mountains may depart and the hills disappear, but even then I will remain loyal to you, <u>Grace</u>. My covenant of blessing will never be broken," says the Lord, who has mercy on you.

ISAIAH 54: 1—10

See how I placed my name, "<u>Grace</u>," into those scriptures of promise. Now, take your name and place it in wherever you see "Grace." God knew what would make me happy, blessed. He promised me my heart's desire before I even knew what would make me happy. And now, I can now look back thirty—three years later, to see God's faithfulness and His promises fulfilled in my life. <u>So be bold and place your name into the Word</u> and make His promises your own heart's desire. In prayer, ask God for a promise or scripture that He wants to fulfill in your life. And wait quietly, listening to your heart. He will answer. Try saying in your heart, "*Lord God, I love you,*" and then <u>listen for His reply</u>. He will answer.

If your need is: children, a husband, a wife, a home, or salvation for your children, take these scriptures in Psalms and Isaiah and place your name in them. There are many, many more promises in God's Word for a family and home. Know that all the promises are yours! Know that God is *thrilled* when we claim one of His promises, because *He wants to love His children*!!!

20. "The Redeemer will come to Jerusalem," says the Lord, "to buy back those in Israel who have turned from their sins. 21. And this is my covenant with them," says the Lord. "My Spirit will not leave them, and neither will these words I have given you. They will be on your lips and on the lips of your children and your children's children forever. I, the Lord, have spoken!

ISAIAH 59: 20, 21

Ephesians 5: 1, 2

Follow God's example in everything you do, because you are his dear children. 2. Live a life filled with love for others following the example of Christ, who loved you and gave himself as a sacrifice to take away your sins. And God was pleased, because that sacrifice was like sweet perfume to him.

Romans 8: 31—39

31. What can we say about such wonderful things as these? If God is for us, who can ever be against us? 32. Since God did not spare even his own Son but gave him up for us all, won't God, who gave us Christ, also give us everything else?

33. Who dares accuse us whom God has chosen for his own? Will God? No! He is the one who has given us right standing with himself. 34. Who then will condemn us? Will Christ Jesus? No, for he is the one who died for us and was raised to life for us and is sitting at the place of highest honor next to God, pleading for us.

35. Can anything ever separate us from Christ's love? Does it mean he no longer loves us if we have trouble or calamity, or are persecuted, or are hungry or cold or in danger or threatened with death? 36. (Even the Scriptures say, "For your sake we are killed every day; we are being slaughtered like sheep.") 37. No, despite all these things, overwhelming victory is ours through Christ, who loved us.

38. And I am convinced that nothing can ever separate us from his love. Death can't, and life can't. The angels can't, and the demons can't. Our fears for today, our worries about tomorrow, and even the powers of hell can't keep God's love away. 39. Whether we are high above the sky or in the deepest ocean, nothing in all creation will ever be able to separate us from the love of God that is revealed in Christ Jesus our Lord.

THE APOSTLE PAUL

"70 x 7" Jesus

Prayer for Salvation and Baptism of the Holy Spirit and Fire

Jesus, come into my heart and life. Please make me a new creature, born-again, and I make you my Lord. I ask your forgiveness for all my sin and please baptize me in the Holy Spirit, and fire. Please grant me a heavenly language of prayer, tongues, so that I may praise and worship you in Spirit and in truth. Place a call on my life and grant me guidance and wisdom. May I have strong hope and give hope to all I touch, in word and deed. Open my eyes and heart to the needs all around me and as I unselfishly give to others, meet my needs and heart's desires. Grant me the abundant life that Jesus promised in John 10 and help me to obey your commands of love in your Word. Keep me humble and safe. Grant me the wisdom, grace, deliverance, and power to overcome all the enemies' temptations and deceptions, satan and all his demonic realm. May I live a life of victory and blessing as you promised in Deuteronomy 28: 1—14. Thank you for hearing and answering all of my prayers and heart's cry knowing what I need before even I do."

"In the precious, precious, holy name and blood of Jesus."

"Amen."

_Write today's date here: _____._

Printed in the United States
By Bookmasters